You Can't Catch Me!

Gerald Rose

CAMBRIDGE
UNIVERSITY PRESS

There was a party at Curly's house.

BANG went the balloons. Curly didn't like that.

"It's much too noisy," she said. "I'm getting out of here."

She walked past Bonzo's house. Bonzo
was a big, noisy dog.

"I can smell Bonzo's dinner," said Curly.

Curly crept inside Bonzo's house and
tasted his dinner.

"Mmm! This tastes good," she said.

But then – Bonzo rushed in.
"WOOF! Who's been eating my dinner?"
he barked.

"MEEEEEOW!" said Curly. "I was only
tasting it."

"GRRR! I'll get you," barked Bonzo.

Curly ran into the next room.
"You can't catch me!" she said.

Bonzo ran after her.
"GRRR! I'll get you," he barked.

He jumped after Curly and . . .

CRASH! He landed on the television.

Curly ran upstairs. "You can't catch me!"
said Curly.

"GRRR! I'll get you," barked Bonzo.

They both ran into the bathroom and . . .
SPLASH! Bonzo landed in the water!

Curly ran into a bedroom.
"GRRR! I'll get you," barked Bonzo.

"MEEEEEOW!" said Curly.
She jumped out of the window and . . .

. . . landed on top of a van!

Bonzo jumped out of the window too.
But *he* landed in the road!

Curly laughed. "No-one ever catches Curly the cat," she said.

The van drove past Curly's house and she jumped off.

When she got in, the party was over.
The house was quiet.
"I can smell dinner," said Curly.

There was cream in one of her bowls, and chicken in the other.

"You can't catch me!" said Curly.